MCRP 6-12D

# Devotional Field Book

US Marine Corps

DISTRIBUTION STATEMENT A: Approved for public release; distribution is unlimited.

PCN 144 000142 00

## To Our Readers

**Changes:** Readers of this publication are encouraged to submit suggestions and changes that will improve it. Recommendations may be sent directly to Commanding General, Marine Corps Combat Development Command, Doctrine Division (C 42), 3300 Russell Road, Suite 318A, Quantico, VA 22134-5021 or by fax to 703-784-2917 (DSN 278-2917) or by E-mail to **nancy.morgan@usmc.mil**. Recommendations should include the following information:

- Location of change
    Publication number and title
    Current page number
    Paragraph number (if applicable)
    Line number
    Figure or table number (if applicable)
- Nature of change
    Add, delete
    Proposed new text, preferably double-spaced and typewritten
- Justification and/or source of change

**Additional copies:** A printed copy of this publication may be obtained from Marine Corps Logistics Base, Albany, GA 31704-5001, by following the instructions in MCBul 5600, *Marine Corps Doctrinal Publications Status.* An electronic copy may be obtained from the Doctrine Division, MCCDC, world wide web home page which is found at the following universal reference locator: **https://www.doctrine.usmc.mil**.

Unless otherwise stated, whenever the masculine gender is used, both men and women are included.

DEPARTMENT OF THE NAVY
Headquarters United States Marine Corps
Washington, D.C. 20380-1775

6 February 2004

## FOREWORD

Marine Corps Reference Publication 6-12D, *Devotional Field Book*, is a resource for Command Religious Programs (CRPs) in the Marine Corps. In addition to being a personal devotional guide for Marines and Sailors, it may be used in conducting divine services or lay led services. This book has been designed primarily to support those operations where limited printed resources are available for the CRP.

The scriptures, prayers, hymns, songs, statements of faith and meditations contained in this book were carefully chosen by chaplains, Marines, and Sailors. These selections have historically offered guidance, encouragement, and support to people in time of need.

This book supersedes Navy Marine Corps (NAVMC) 2765. It is dedicated to the hope that it will lead others to the inexhaustible resources of God.

Reviewed and approved this date.

BY DIRECTION OF THE COMMANDANT OF THE MARINE CORPS

EDWARD HANLON, JR.
Lieutenant General, U.S. Marine Corps
Commanding General
Marine Corps Combat Development Command

Publication Control Number: 14400014200

DISTRIBUTION STATEMENT A: Approved for public release; distribution is unlimited.

# THE MARINE'S PRAYER

Almighty Father, whose command is over all and whose love never fails, make me aware of thy presence and obedient to thy will. Keep me true to my best self, guarding me against dishonesty in purpose and deed, and helping me to live so that I can face my fellow Marines, my loved ones, and thee without shame or fear. Protect my family. Give me the will to do the work of a Marine and to accept my share of responsibilities with vigor and enthusiasm. Grant me the courage to be proficient in my daily performance. Keep me loyal and faithful to my superiors and to the duties my country and the Marine Corps have entrusted to me. Make me considerate of those committed to my leadership. Help me to wear my uniform with dignity, and let it remind me daily of the traditions which I must uphold.

If I am inclined to doubt, steady my faith; if I am tempted, make me strong to resist; if I should miss the mark, give me courage to try again.

Guide me with the light of truth and grant me wisdom by which I may understand the answer to my prayer. Amen

The United States Marine Corps is indebted to all who gave permission to use worship materials, hymns, and tunes under their control that are used in this Devotional Field Book. Every effort was made to ensure that all copyrighted works are used by permission of the owners.

Acknowledgement of such permission is given in the index of acknowledgements and sources or below the hymns, as appropriate. If, through oversight, any copyrighted material has been used without permission, proper acknowledgement will be given in future printings. Reproduction of copyrighted material is not authorized without permission of the copyright owners.

# CONTENTS

## SCRIPTURES
| | |
|---|---|
| Hebrew/Old Testament............. | 1 |
| New Testament .................. | 16 |

## STATEMENTS OF FAITH
| | |
|---|---|
| Christian........................ | 29 |
| Jewish ......................... | 31 |

## PRAYERS
| | |
|---|---|
| General ........................ | 32 |
| Roman Catholic .................. | 39 |
| Orthodox ....................... | 44 |
| Jewish ......................... | 44 |
| Islam........................... | 49 |
| Buddhist Meditation ............... | 50 |

## LYRICS TO HYMNS
| | |
|---|---|
| Christian........................ | 51 |
| Jewish ......................... | 71 |
| Patriotic ....................... | 75 |

## REFLECTIONS

## REFERENCES

# SCRIPTURES

### Hebrew/Old Testament

*Exodus 20*

And God spoke all these words,
**2** "I am the LORD your God, who brought you out of the land of Egypt, out of the land of slavery.
**3** "You shall have no other gods before me.
**4** "You shall not make for yourself an idol in the form of anything in heaven above or on the earth beneath or in the waters below.
**5** You shall not bow down to them or worship them; for I, the LORD your God, am a jealous God, punishing the children for the sin of the fathers to the third and the fourth generation of those who hate me,
**6** but showing love to a thousand generations of those who love me and keep my commandments.
**7** "You shall not misuse the name of the LORD your God, for the LORD will not hold anyone guiltless who misuses his name.
**8** "Remember the Sabbath day by keeping it holy.
**9** Six days you shall labor, and do all your work,
**10** but the seventh day is a Sabbath to the LORD

your God. On it you shall not do any work neither you nor your son or daughter, nor your manservant, or maidservant, nor your animals, nor the alien within your gates.

**11** For in six days the LORD made the heavens and the earth, the sea, and all that is in them, but he rested the seventh day. Therefore the LORD blessed the Sabbath day and made it holy.

**12** "Honor your father and your mother, that your days may be long in the land which the LORD your God is giving you.

**13** "You shall not murder.

**14** "You shall not commit adultery.

**15** "You shall not steal.

**16** "You shall not bear false testimony against your neighbor.

**17** "You shall not covet your neighbor's house. You shall not covet your neighbor's wife, or his manservant, or his maidservant, his ox or his donkey, or anything that belongs to your neighbor."

## *Deuteronomy 10*

**12** "And now, Israel, what does the LORD your God ask of you, but to fear the LORD your God, to walk in all his ways, to love him, to serve the

LORD your God with all your heart and with all your soul,

**13** and to observe the LORD's commands and decrees that I am giving you today for your own good?

**14** To the LORD your God belong the heavens, even the highest heavens, the earth and everything in it.

**15** Yet the LORD set his affection on your forefathers and loved them, and he chose you, their descendants, above all the nations as it is today.

**16** Circumcise your hearts, therefore, and do not be stiff-necked any longer.

**17** For the LORD your God is God of gods and LORD of lords, the great God, mighty and awesome, who shows no partiality and accepts no bribes.

**18** He defends the cause of the fatherless and the widow, and loves the alien, giving him food and clothing.

**19** And you are to love those who are aliens, for you yourselves were aliens in Egypt.

**20** Fear the LORD your God and serve him. Hold fast to him and take your oaths in his name.

**21** He is your praise; he is your God, who performed for you those great and awesome wonders you saw with your own eyes.

**22** Your forefathers who went down into Egypt were seventy in all, and now the LORD your God has made you as numerous as the stars in the sky.

### *Joshua 1*

**9** Have I not commanded you? Be strong and courageous. Do not be terrified; do not be discouraged, for the LORD your God will be with you wherever you go."

### *Proverbs 3*

**5** Trust in the LORD with all your heart, and lean not on your own understanding;

**6** in all your ways acknowledge him, and he will make your paths straight.

### *Psalm 1*

**1** Blessed is the man who does not walk in the counsel of the wicked or stand in the way of sinners or sit in the seat of mockers.

**2** But his delight is in the law of the Lord, and on his law he meditates day and night.

**3** He is like a tree planted by streams of water, which yields its fruit in season and whose leaf does not wither. Whatever he does prospers.

**4** Not so wicked! They are like chaff that the wind blows away.

**5** Therefore the wicked will not stand in the judgment, nor sinners in the assembly of the righteous.

**6** For the Lord watches over the way of the righteous, but the way of the wicked will perish.

### *Psalm 23*

**1** The LORD is my shepherd, I shall not be in want;

**2** He makes me lie down in green pastures. He leads me beside quiet waters;

**3** he restores my soul. He guides me in paths of righteousness for his name's sake.

**4** Even though I walk through the valley of the shadow of death, I will fear no evil, for you are with me; your rod and your staff, they comfort me.

**5** You prepare a table before me in the presence of my enemies. You anoint my head with oil; my cup overflows.

**6** Surely goodness and mercy will follow me all the days of my life, and I will dwell in the house of the LORD forever.

### *Psalm 24*

**1** The earth is the LORD's, and everything in it, the world, and all who live in it;

**2** for he founded it upon the seas and established it upon the waters.

**3** Who may ascend the hill of the LORD? Who may stand in his holy place?

**4** He who has clean hands and a pure heart, who does not lift up his soul to an idol or swear by what is false.

**5** He will receive blessing from the LORD and vindication from God his Savior.

**6** Such is the generation of those who seek him, who seek your face, O God of Jacob.

## *Psalm 46*

**1** God is our refuge and strength, an ever-present help in trouble.

**2** Therefore we will not fear, though the earth give way and the mountains fall into the heart of the sea,

**3** though its waters roar and foam and the mountains quake with their surging.

**4** There is a river whose streams make glad the city of God, the holy place where the Most High dwells.

**5** God is within her, she will not fall; God will help her at break of day.

**6** Nations are in uproar, kingdoms fall; he lifts his voice, the earth melts.

**7** The LORD Almighty is with us; the God of Jacob is our fortress.

**8** Come, and see the works of the LORD, the desolations he has brought on the earth.

**9** He makes wars cease to the ends of the earth; he breaks the bow, and shatters the spear, he burns the shields with fire.

**10** "Be still, and know that I am God; I will be exalted among the nations, I will be exalted in the earth."

**11** The LORD Almighty is with us; the God of Jacob is our fortress.

## *Psalm 91*

**1** He who dwells in the shelter of the Most High will rest in the shadow of the Almighty.

**2** I will say of the LORD, "He is my refuge and my fortress, my God, in whom I trust."

**3** Surely he will save you from the fowler's snare and from the deadly pestilence.

**4** He will cover you with his feathers, and under his wings you will find refuge; his faithfulness will be your shield and rampart.

**5** You will not fear the terror of night, nor the arrow that flies by day,

**6** nor the pestilence that stalks in the darkness, nor the plague that destroys at midday.

**7** A thousand may fall at your side, ten thousand at your right hand, but it will not come near you.

**8** You will only observe with your eyes and see the punishment of the wicked.

**9** If you make the Most High your dwelling—even the LORD, who is my refuge—

**10** then no harm will befall you, no disaster will come near your tent.

**11** For he will command his angels concerning you to guard you in all your ways;

**12** they will lift you up in their hands, so that you will not strike your food against a stone.

**13** You will tread upon the lion and the cobra; you will trample the great lion and the serpent.

**14** "Because he loves me," says the LORD, "I will rescue him; I will protect him, for he acknowledges my name.

**15** He will call upon me, and I will answer him; I will be with him in trouble, I will deliver him and honor him.

**16** With long life will I satisfy him and show him my salvation."

## *Psalm 100*

**1** Shout for joy to the LORD, all the earth.

**2** Worship the LORD with gladness; come before him with joyful songs.

**3** Know that the LORD is God. It is he who made us, and we are his; we are his people, the sheep of his pasture.

**4** Enter his gates with thanksgiving and his courts with praise; give thanks to him and praise his name.

**5** For the LORD is good and his love endures forever; his faithfulness continues through all generations.

## *Psalm 121*

**1** I lift up my eyes to the hills—where does my help come from?

**2** My help comes from the LORD, the Maker of heaven and earth.

**3** He will not let your foot slip—he who watches over you will not slumber;

**4** indeed, he who watches over Israel will neither slumber nor sleep.

**5** The LORD watches over you—the LORD is your shade at the right hand;

**6** the sun will not harm you by day, nor the moon by night.

**7** The LORD will keep you from all harm—he will watch over your life.

**8** The LORD will watch over your coming and going both now and forevermore.

## *Psalm 130*

**1** Out of the depths I cry to you, O LORD;

**2** O LORD, hear my voice. Let your ears be attentive to my cry for mercy.

**3** If you, O LORD, kept a record of sins, O LORD, who could stand?

**4** But with you there is forgiveness; therefore you are feared.

**5** I wait for the LORD, my soul waits, and in his word I put my hope.

**6** My soul waits for the Lord more than watchmen wait for the morning, more than watchmen wait for the morning.

**7** O Israel, put your hope in the LORD, for with the LORD is unfailing love and with him is full redemption.

**8** He himself will redeem Israel from all their sins.

*Psalm 139*

**1** O LORD, you have searched me and you know me.

**2** You know when I sit and when I rise; you perceive my thoughts from afar.

**3** You discern my going out and my lying down; you are familiar with all my ways.

**4** Before a word is on my tongue you know it completely, O LORD.

**5** You hem me in—behind and before; you have laid your hand upon me.

**6** Such knowledge is too wonderful for me, too lofty for me to attain.

**7** Where can I go from your Spirit? Where can I flee from your presence?

**8** If I go up to the heavens, you are there; if I make my bed in the depths, you are there.

**9** If I rise on the wings of the dawn, if I settle on the far side of the sea,

**10** even there your hand will guide me, your right hand will hold me fast.

**11** If I say, "Surely the darkness will hide me and the light become night around me,"

**12** even the darkness will not be dark to you; the night will shine like the day, for darkness is as light to you.

**13** For you created my inmost being; you knit me together in my mother's womb.

**14** I praise you because I am fearfully and wonderfully made; your works are wonderful, I know that full well.

**15** My frame was not hidden from you when I was made in the secret place. When I was woven together in the depths of the earth,

**16** your eyes saw my unformed body. All the days ordained for me were written in your book before one of them came to be.

**17** How precious to me are your thoughts, O God! How vast is the sum of them!

**18** Were I to count them, they would outnumber the grains of sand. When I awake, I am still with you.

**19** If only you would slay the wicked O God! Away from me, you bloodthirsty men!

**20** They speak of you with evil intent; your adversaries misuse your name.

**21** Do I not hate those who hate you, O LORD, and abhor those who rise up against you?

**22** I have nothing but hatred for them; I count them my enemies.

**23** Search me, O God, and know my heart; test me and know my anxious thoughts.

**24** See if there is any offensive way in me, and lead me in the way everlasting.

### *Psalm 150*

**1** Praise the LORD. Praise God in his sanctuary; praise him in his mighty heavens.

**2** Praise him for his acts of power; praise him for his surpassing greatness.

**3** Praise him with the sounding of the trumpet, praise him with the harp and lyre,

**4** praise him with tambourine and dancing, praise him with the strings and flute,

**5** praise him with the clash of cymbals, praise him with resounding cymbals.

**6** Let everything that has breath praise the LORD. Praise the LORD.

## NEW TESTAMENT

### *Matthew 5*

**1** Now when he saw the crowds, he went up on a mountainside and sat down. His disciples came to him,

**2** and he began to teach them saying:

**3** "Blessed are the poor in spirit, for theirs is the kingdom of heaven.

**4** Blessed are those who mourn, for they will be comforted.

**5** Blessed are the meek, for they will inherit the earth.

**6** Blessed are those who hunger and thirst for righteousness, for they will be filled.

**7** Blessed are the merciful, for they will be shown mercy.

**8** Blessed are the pure in heart, for they will see God.

**9** Blessed are the peacemakers, for they will be called sons of God.

**10** Blessed are those who are persecuted because of righteousness, for theirs is the kingdom of heaven.

**11** "Blessed are you when people insult you, persecute you and falsely say all kinds of evil against you because of me.

**12** Rejoice and be glad, because great is your reward in heaven, for in the same way they persecuted the prophets who were before you.

### *John 3*

**16** For God so love the world that he gave his one and only Son, that whoever believes in him shall not perish but have eternal life.

**17** For God did not sent his Son into the world to condemn the world, but to save the world through him.

**18** Whoever believes in him is not condemned, but whoever does not believe stands condemned already because he has not believed in the name of God's one and only Son.

## *John 14*

**1** "Do not let your hearts be troubled. Trust in God, trust also in me.

**2** In my Father's house are many rooms; if it were not so, I would have told you. I am going there to prepare a place for you.

**3** And if I go and prepare a place for you, I will come back and take you to be with me that you also may be where I am.

**4** You know the way to the place where I am going."

**5** Thomas said to him, "Lord, we don't know where you are going, so how can we know the way?"

**6** Jesus answered, "I am the way and the truth and the life. No one comes to the Father except through me."

## *Romans 8*

**31** What, then, shall we say in response to this? If God is for us, who can be against us?

**32** He who did not spare his own Son, but gave him up for us all—how will he not also, along with him, graciously give us all things?

**33** Who will bring any charge against those whom God has chosen? It is God who justifies.

**34** Who is he that condemns? Christ Jesus, who died—more than that, who was raised to life—is at the right hand of God and is also interceding for us.

**35** Who shall separate us from the love of Christ? Shall trouble or hardship or persecution or famine or nakedness or danger or sword?

**36** As it is written: "For your sake we face death all day long; we are considered as sheep to be slaughtered."

**37** No, in all these things we are more than conquerors through him who loved us.

**38** For I am convinced that neither death nor life, neither angels nor demons, neither the present nor the future, nor any powers,

**39** neither height nor depth, nor anything else in all creation, will be able to separate us from the love of God that is in Christ Jesus our Lord.

## *Romans 12*

**9** Love must be sincere. Hate what is evil; cling to what is good.

**10** Be devoted to one another in brotherly love. Honor one another above yourselves.

**11** Never be lacking in zeal, but keep your spiritual fervor, serving the Lord.

**12** Be joyful in hope, patient in affliction, faithful in prayer.

**13** Share with God's people who are in need. Practice hospitality.

**14** Bless those who persecute you; bless and do not curse.

**15** Rejoice with those who rejoice; mourn with those who mourn.

**16** Live in harmony with one another. Do not be proud, but be willing to associate with people of low position. Do not be conceited.

**17** Do not repay anyone evil for evil. Be careful to do what is right in the eyes of everybody.

**18** If it is possible, as far as it depends on you, live at peace with everyone.

**19** Do not take revenge, my friends, but leave room for God's wrath, for it is written: "It is mine to avenge; I will repay," says the Lord.

**20** On the contrary: "If your enemy is hungry, feed him; if he is thirsty, give him something to drink. In doing this, you will heap burning coals on his head."

**21** Do not overcome by evil, but overcome evil with good.

*1 Corinthians 13*

**1** If I speak in the tongues of men and of angels, but have not love, I am only a resounding gong or a clanging cymbal.

**2** If I have the gift of prophecy and can fathom all mysteries and all knowledge, and if I have a faith that can move mountains, but have not love, I am nothing.

**3** If I give all I possess to the poor and surrender my body to the flames, but have not love, I gain nothing.

**4** Love is patient, love is kind. It does not envy, it does not boast, it is not proud.

**5** It is not rude, it is not self-seeking, it is not easily angered, it keeps no record of wrongs.

**6** Love does not delight in evil but rejoices with the truth.

**7** It always protects, always trusts, always hopes, always perseveres.

**8** Love never fails. But where there are prophecies, they will cease; where there are tongues, they will be stilled; where there is knowledge, it will pass away.

**9** For we know in part and we prophesy in part,

**10** but when perfection comes, the imperfect disappears.

**11** When I was a child, I talked like a child, I thought like a child, I reasoned like a child. When I became a man, I put childish ways behind me.

**12** Now we see but a poor reflection as in a mirror; then we shall see face to face. Now I know in part; then I shall know fully, even as I am fully known.

**13** And now these three remain: faith, hope and love. But the greatest of these is love.

## *1 Corinthians 15*

**12** But if it is preached that Christ has been raised from the dead, how can some of you say that there is no resurrection of the dead?

**13** If there is no resurrection of the dead, then not even Christ has been raised.

**14** And if Christ has not been raised, our preaching is useless and so is your faith.

**15** More than that, we are then found to be false witnesses about God, for we have testified about God that he raised Christ from the dead. But he did not raise him if in fact the dead are not raised.

**16** For if the dead are not raised, then Christ has not been raised either.

**17** And if Christ has not been raised, your faith is futile; you are still in your sins.

**18** Then those also who have fallen asleep in Christ are lost.

**19** If only for this life we have hope in Christ, we are to be pitied more than all men.

**20** But Christ has indeed been raised from the dead, the firstfruits of those who have fallen asleep.

**21** For since death came through a man, the resurrection of the dead comes also through a man.

### *Ephesians 6*

**10** Finally, be strong in the Lord and in his mighty power.

**11** Put on the full armor of God so that you can take your stand against the devil's schemes.

**12** For our struggle is not against flesh and blood, but against the rulers, against the authorities, against the powers of this dark world and against the spiritual forces of evil in the heavenly realms.

**13** Therefore put on the full armor of God, so that when the day of evil comes, you may be able to stand your ground, and after you have done everything, to stand.

**14** Stand firm then, with the belt of truth buckled around your waist, with the breastplate of righteousness in place,

**15** and with your feet fitted with the readiness that comes from the gospel of peace.

**16** In addition to all this, take up the shield of faith, with which you can extinguish all the flaming arrows of the evil one.

**17** Take the helmet of salvation and the sword of the Spirit, which is the word of God.

**18** And pray in the Spirit on all occasions with all kinds of prayers and requests. With this in mind, be alert and always keep on praying for all the saints.

## *Philippians 4*

**5** Let your gentleness be evident to all. The Lord is near.

**6** Do not be anxious about anything, but in everything, by prayer and petition, with thanksgiving, present your request to God.

**7** And the peace of God, which transcends all understanding, will guard your hearts and your minds in Christ Jesus.

**8** Finally, brothers, whatever is true, whatever is noble, whatever is right, whatever is pure, whatever is lovely, whatever is admirable—if anything is excellent or praiseworthy—think about such things.

**9** Whatever you have learned or received or heard from me, or seen in me—put it into practice. And the God of peace will be with you.

**10** I rejoice greatly in the Lord that at least you have renewed your concern for me. Indeed, you have been concerned, but you had no opportunity to show it.

**11** I am not saying this because I am in need, for I have learned to be content whatever the circumstances.

**12** I know what it is to be in need, and I know what it is to have plenty. I have learned the secret of being content in any and every situation, whether well fed or hungry, whether living in plenty or in want.

**13** I can do everything through him who gives me strength.

*1 John 3*

**14** We know that we have passed from death to life, because we love our brothers. Anyone who does not love remains in death.

**15** Anyone who hates his brother is a murderer, and you know that no murderer has eternal life in him.

**16** This is how we know what love is: Jesus Christ laid down his life for us. And we ought to lay down our lives for our brothers.

**17** If anyone has material possessions and sees his brother in need but has no pity on him, how can the love of God be in him?

**18** Dear children, let us not love with words or tongue but with actions and in truth.

# STATEMENTS OF FAITH

### CHRISTIAN

## *The Apostolic Creed*

I believe in God, the Father Almighty, creator of heaven and earth. I believe in Jesus Christ, his only Son, our Lord. He was conceived by the power of the Holy Spirit and born of the Virgin Mary. He suffered under Pontius Pilate, was crucified, died and was buried. He decended to the dead. On the third day he rose again.

He ascended into heaven, and is seated at the right hand of the Father. He will come again to judge the living and the dead. I believe in the Holy Spirit, the holy catholic church, the communion of saints, the forgiveness of sins, the resurrection of the body, and the life everlasting. Amen.

## *The Nicene Creed*

We believe in one God, the Father, the Almighty, maker of heaven and earth, of all that is seen and unseen. We believe in one Lord, Jesus Christ, the only Son of God, eternally begotten of the Father,

God from God, Light from Light, true God from true God, begotten, not made, one in being with the Father. Through him all things were made. For us and for our salvation he came down from heaven: by the power of the Holy Spirit he was born of the Virgin Mary, and became man. For our sake he was crucified under Pontius Pilate; he suffered, died and was buried. On the third day, he rose again in fulfillment of the Scriptures: he ascended into heaven and is seated at the right hand of the Father. He will come again in glory to judge the living and the dead, and his kingdom will have no end.

We believe in the Holy Spirit, the Lord, the giver of life, who proceeds from the Father and the Son. With the Father and the Son he is worshipped and glorified. He has spoken through the prophets. We believe in one holy catholic and apostolic church. We acknowledge one baptism for the forgiveness of sins. We look for the resurrection of the dead, and the life of the world to come. Amen.

## JEWISH

I am a Jew because the faith of Israel demands of me no abdication of my mind. I am a Jew because the faith of Israel asks every possible sacrifice of my soul. I am a Jew because in all places where there are tears and suffering the Jew weeps. I am a Jew because in every age when the cry of despair is heard the Jew hopes. I am a Jew because the message of Israel is the most ancient and the most modern. I am a Jew because Israel's promise is a universal promise. I am a Jew because for Israel the world is not finished; men will complete it. I am a Jew because for Israel man is not yet fully created; men are creating him. I am a Jew because Israel places man and his unity above nations and above Israel itself. I am a Jew because above man, image of the divine unity, Israel places the unity which is divine.

—Edmund Fleg

# PRAYERS

## GENERAL

### *The Lord's Prayer*

Our Father who art in heaven, hallowed be thy name. Thy kingdom come, thy will be done, on earth as it is in heaven. Give us this day our daily bread; and forgive us our debts, as we also have forgiven our debtors; and lead us not into temptation, but deliver us from evil. Amen. (*For thine is the kingdom and the power and the glory, forever.)

* Protestant

### *My Morning Offering*

O God, for another day, for another morning, for another hour, for another minute, for another chance to live and serve you, I am truly grateful.

Do you this day free me from all fear of the future, from all anxiety about tomorrow, from all bitterness towards anyone, from all cowardice in the face of danger, from all laziness in the face of work, from all failure before opportunity, from all weakness when your power is at hand.

But fill me with love that knows no barrier, with sympathy that reaches to all, with courage that cannot be shaken, with faith strong enough for the darkness, with strength sufficient for my tasks, with loyalty to your kingdom's goal, with wisdom to meet life's complexities, with power to lift me to you.

Be with me for another day, and use me as you will. Amen.

### *Prayer of St. Francis of Assisi*

Lord, make me an instrument of your peace. Where there is hatred, let me sow love; where there is injury, pardon; where there is doubt, faith; where there is despair, hope; where there is darkness, light; and where there is sadness, joy. O Divine Master, grant that I may not so much seek to be consoled as to console; to be understood as to understand; to be loved as to love. For it is in giving that we receive; it is in pardoning that we are pardoned; and it is in dying that we are born to eternal life.

### *For Team Spirit*

God, our Father, give us all a sense of cooperation. Help us realize that we can't exist alone. Leaders need men and men need leaders. Make us sense our basic unity of purpose. Help us see that individual welfare is intimately tied to the welfare of the whole group, and that the whole group depends upon the well-being of the individual. Help us see this and above all help us to live out this insight. Amen.

### *Self-Dedication*

Almighty God, draw our hearts to you, guide our minds, fill our imaginations, control our wills, so that we may be wholly yours. Use us as you will, always to your glory and the welfare of your people. Amen.

### *For Those in Our Country's Service in Time of War*

Almighty God, our heavenly Father, let thy protection be upon all those who are in the service of our country; guard them from all harm and danger of body and soul; sustain and comfort those at home, especially in their hours of loneliness, anxiety, and sorrow; prepare the dying for death and the living for thy service; give success to our arms on land and sea and in the air; and grant unto us and all nations a speedy, just and lasting peace. Amen.

God, grant me serenity to accept the things I cannot change, courage to change the things I can, and wisdom to know the difference. Living one day at a time; enjoying one moment at a time; accepting hardship as a pathway to peace taking as Jesus did, this sinful world as it is, not as I would have it.

Trusting that you will make all things right if I surrender to your will; that I may be reasonably happy in this life, and supremely happy with you forever in the next. Amen.

—Reinhold Niebuhr

God of love and peace, sometimes we are trapped in situations when war is inevitable and we are called to fight to defend those things we hold dear. Help us to enter into such situations remembering your charge to love our enemies, to do good to those who curse us, and to pray for those who abuse us. Keep us mindful of these things, O Lord. In Jesus' name, Amen.

—Eli Fisher

Loving Christ, your call to love our enemies challenges us.

Sometimes we fail. Teach us to love in ways that transform hate. Amen.

—George Graham

I am no longer my own but yours. Put me to what you will, rank me with whoever you will, put me to doing...Put me to suffering. Let me be empowered for you, or laid aside for you, exulted for you, or brought low for you. Let me be full, let me be empty.

Let me have all things. Let me have nothing. I freely and wholeheartly yield all things to your pleasure and disposal. And now, glorious and blessed God, Father, Son and Holy Spirit, you are mine and I am yours. So be it. And this Covenant, now made on earth, let it be ratified in heaven. Amen.

—John Wesley

It helps, now and then, to step back and take a long view.

The kingdom is not only beyond our efforts, it is even beyond our vision.

We may never see the end results, but that is the difference between the master builder and the worker.

We are prophets of a future not our own. Amen.

—Archbishop Oscar Romero

Dear God, I have no idea where I am going.

I do not see the road ahead of me.

I cannot know for certain where it will end.

But I believe this:

I believe the desire to please you does in fact please you.

I hope I have that desire in everything I do.

I hope I never persist in anything apart from that desire.

Therefore I will trust you always, for though I may be lost—and in the shadow of death—I will not be afraid, because I know you will never leave me to face my troubles all alone.

—Thomas Merton

In comparison with this big world, the human heart is only a small thing.

Though the world is so large, it is utterly unable to satisfy this tiny heart.

The ever-growing soul and its capacity can be satisfied only in you, Infinite God. As water is restless until it reaches its level, so the soul has not peace until it rests in you.

—Sundar Singh

O Great Spirit, whose breath gives life to the world,
And whose voice is heard in the soft breeze:

We need your strength and wisdom.

Cause us to walk in beauty, give us eyes ever to behold the red and purple sunset.

Make us wise so that we may understand what you have taught us.

—Native American Prayer

## ROMAN CATHOLIC

### *Our Father*

Our Father, who art in heaven, hallowed be thy name; thy Kingdom come, thy will be done on earth as it is in heaven. Give us this day our daily bread; and forgive us our trespasses as we forgive those who trespass against us; and lead us not into temptation, but deliver us from evil. Amen.

### *Hail Mary*

Hail Mary, full of grace. The Lord is with thee. Blessed art thou amongst women, and blessed is the fruit of thy womb, Jesus.

Holy Mary, Mother of God, pray for us sinners, now and at the hour of our death. Amen.

### *The Rosary*

**The Joyful Mysteries**

- The messenger of God announces to Mary that she is to be the Mother of God.
- Mary visits and helps her cousin Elizabeth.
- Mary gives birth to Jesus in a stable in Bethlehem.

- Jesus is presented in the temple.
- Jesus is found in the temple.

### The Sorrowful Mysteries

- Jesus undergoes his agony in the Garden of Gethsemane.
- Jesus is scourged at the pillar.
- Jesus is crowned with thorns.
- Jesus carries the cross to Calvary.
- Jesus dies on the cross for our sins.

### The Glorious Mysteries

- Jesus rises from the dead.
- Jesus ascends into heaven.
- The Holy Spirit comes to the apostles and the Blessed Mother.
- The Mother of Jesus is taken into heaven.
- Mary is crowned queen of heaven and earth.

### Luminous Mysteries

- The Baptism of Jesus.
- The Wedding at Cana.
- The proclamation of the Kingdom of God.
- The Transfiguration.
- The Institution of the Eucharist.

**Stations of the Cross**

(At each station, contemplate the scene and pray a brief, heartfelt prayer.)

- Jesus is condemned to death on the cross. (Mark 14:61-64)
- Jesus accepts his cross. (John 19:14-17)
- Jesus falls the first time. (John 15:18-20)
- Jesus meets his sorrowful Mother. (John 19:25-27)
- Simon of Cyrene helps Jesus carry his cross. (Mark 15:20-22)
- Veronica wipes the face of Jesus. (Matthew 25:37-40)
- Jesus falls the second time. (Isaiah 53:4-6)
- Jesus meets and speaks to the women of Jerusalem. (Luke 23:27-28)
- Jesus falls the third time. (Psalm 118:25-28)
- Jesus is stripped of his garments. (Matthew 27:34-35)
- Jesus is nailed to the cross. (Luke 23:33-34)
- Jesus dies on the cross. (Luke 23:44-46)
- Jesus is taken down from the cross and laid in his Mother's arms. (John 19:33-37)

- Jesus is placed in the tomb. (Matthew 27:59-60)
- Jesus rises from the dead. (Mark 16:1-6)

**Evening Prayer**

O God of all love, when will we truly believe that you do love us beyond our understanding? Each day tells it to the other as each offers us your precious gifts. Each night would speak it anew to us as you give us rest and renewal. But the greatest witness to your love we hear constantly from your Word. There you tell us that your Son shed His blood for us that we might be cleansed from all our sin. Now we can call you "Father." Now we can stand before you in the purity of Christ's righteousness and in the certainty of being your children. Let your love in Christ be the power of our lives and the joys of all our days. We thank you that we can lie down in peace and entrust ourselves to your never-failing love. We rest in Jesus' name. Amen.

**Act of Contrition**

O my God, I am heartily sorry for having offended you, and I detest all my sins because of your just punishments, but most of all because they offend you, my God, who are all-good and deserving of all my love. I firmly resolve, with the help of your grace, to sin no more, and to avoid the near occasions of sin.

**Christopher Prayer**

Father, grant that I might be a bearer of Christ Jesus, your Son. Allow me to warm the often cold, impersonal scene of modern life with your burning love. Strengthen me by your Holy Spirit to carry out my mission of changing the world, or some definite part of it for the better. Despite my lamentable failures, bring home to me that my advantages are your blessings to be shared with others.

Make me more energetic in setting right what I find wrong with the world, instead of complaining about it. Nourish in me a practical desire to build up, rather than to tear down, to reconcile instead of polarize, to go out on a limb rather than crave security. Never let me forget that it is far better to light one candle than to curse the darkness, and to join my light, one day, with yours. Amen.

## ORTHODOX

O Heavenly King, the Comforter, the Spirit of truth who art everywhere and fillest all things. Treasury of Blessings, and Giver of Life: Come and abide in us, and cleanse us from every impurity, and save our souls, O Good One.

O most Holy Trinity, have mercy on us. O Lord, cleanse us from our sins. O Master, pardon our transgressions. O Holy One, visit and heal our infirmities, for thy name's sake.

## JEWISH

### *Barechu*

Bless the Lord, to whom our praise is due.

Ba-re-chu et A-do-nai ha-me-vo-rach.

Blessed be the Lord, to whom our praise is due, now and forever.

Ba-ruch A-do-nai ha-me-vo-rach le-o-lam va-ed.

## *Shema*

Hear, O Israel:

The Lord is our God; the Lord is One!

She-ma Yis-ra-eil:

A-do-nai e-lo-hei-nu; A-do-nai E-chad!

Blessed is his glorious kingdom forever and ever!

You shall love the Lord your God with all your heart, with all your soul, with all your might. Set these words that I command you this day upon your heart. Teach them faithfully to your children; speak of them in your home and on your way, when you lie down and when you rise up. Bind them as a sign upon your hand; let them be a symbol before your eyes; inscribe them on the doorposts of your house and on your gates.

## *Prayer on Starting a Journey*

May it be your will, Lord my God and God of my ancestors, to lead me on the way of peace and guide and direct my steps in peace, so that you will bring me happily to my destination safe and sound. Save me from danger on the way. Give me good grace, kindness, and favor, both in your eyes and in the eyes of all whom I may meet. Hear this my prayer, for you are a God who listens to the heart's request. Fulfill for me your words, "Behold I am sending before you an angel to guard you on the way and to bring you to the place which I have prepared." Blessed are you, O Lord, who hearkens to prayer.

## *Confession for the Critically Ill*

Lord my God and God of my ancestors I acknowledge that in your hand alone is my recovery of my death. May it be your will that I be completely healed. Yet if it be your will that I die, then I shall accept my death lovingly at your hands. May my death be my atonement for all the sins, transgressions, and wrongs that I have done before you. May I receive a portion of that goodness which is stored up for the righteous. Make me to know the path of life, the fullness of blissful joy in your presence at your right hand forevermore.

O you who are the Father of the fatherless and the guardian of the widow, protect my beloved family, whose souls are linked to mine. Into your hand I commend my spirit; you have redeemed me, O God of truth. Amen and Amen.

## *When the End is Approaching*

The Lord is King; the Lord was King; the Lord shall reign forever and ever. (Said three times.)

Blessed is his glorious kingdom forever and ever. (Said three times.)

The Lord, he is God. (Said seven times.)

Hear, O Israel: the Lord is our God; the Lord is One!

She-ma Yis-ra-eil: A-do-nai E-lo-hei-nu; A-do-nai e-chad!

## *Mourner's Kaddish*

May the memory of the departed be a blessing:

Yit-ga-dal ve-yit-ka-dash she-mei ra-ba be-al-ma di-ve-r chi-re-u-tei, ve-yam-lich mal-chu-tei be-cha-yei-chon u-ve-yo-mei-chon u-ve-cha-yei de-chol beit Yis-ra-eil, ba-a-ga-la u-vi-ze-man ka-riv, ve-i-me-ru: a-mein.

Ye-hei she-mei ra-ba me-va-rach le-a-lam u-le-al-mei al-ma-ya.

Yit-ba-rach ve-fish-ta-bach, ve-yit-pa-ar ve-yit-ro-mam ve-yit-na-sei, ve-yit-ha-dar ve-yit-a-leh ve-yit-ha-lal she-mei de-ku-de-sha, be-rich hu, le-ei-la (le-ei-la me-kol) min kol bi-re-cha-ta ve-shi-ra-ta, tush-be-cha-ta ve-ne-che-ma-ta, da-a-mi-ran be-al-ma, ve-I-me-ru: a-mein.

Ye-hei she-la-ma ra-ba min she-ma-ya ve-cha-yim a-lei-nu ve-al kol Yis-ra-eil, ve-I-me-ru: a-mein.

O-se sha-lom bi-me-ro-mav, hu ya-a-he sha-lom altei-nu ve-al kol Yis-ra-eil, ve-i-me-ru: a-mein.

## ISLAM

In the name of God, Most Gracious, Most Merciful.

Praise be to God, the Cherisher and Sustainer of the world; Most Gracious, Most Merciful; Master of the Day of Judgment.

You do we worship, and your aid do we seek.

Show us the straight way.

The way of those on whom you have bestowed your Grace, those whose (portion) is not wrath, and who do not go astray. (Ameen)

(Qur'an Chapter 1: Verses 1-7)

Praise be to God, Lord of the Universe.

There is no deity but God, Most-Forbearing, Supreme in Honor.

Glory be to God, Lord of the Great Throne.

Praise be to God, Lord of the Universe.

I seek of you the means of deserving your mercy, The means of ascertaining your forgiveness, The protection from all mistakes, the benefit from all virtue and the freedom from all sins.

O God! Leave no mistakes, of mine without your forgiveness, nor any stress without your relief, nor any need of which you approve without being fulfilled by you, O Most Merciful of the merciful. (Ameen)

O God! Unto you do I submit, in you do I believe, upon you do I depend, unto you do I turn.

For you do I contend; unto you do I seek judgment.

So forgive me for what I did and will do, for what I concealed and what I declared, and for that of which you are more knowledgeable than me.

Indeed, you are Gracious, Glorious. (Ameen)

## BUDDHIST MEDITATION

The spirit of Buddha is a great compassion and love to save all people by any and all means. It is the spirit of parents toward their children, nourishing and protecting them; it is the spirit that prompts it to be ill with the sickness of people, to suffer with their suffering. "Your suffering is my suffering and your happiness is my happiness," said Buddha, and he does not forget that spirit for a single moment, for it is the self-nature of Buddhahood to be compassionate. A mother realizes her motherhood by loving her child; then the child reacting to its mother's love feels safe and at ease. The Buddha's spirit of compassion is stimulated according to the need of man; man's faith is the reaction to this spirit, and it leads him to enlightenment.

I take refuge in Buddha

I take refuge in Dharma

I take refuge in Sangham

## LYRICS TO HYMNS

### CHRISTIAN

*Lord I Lift Your Name On High*

Lord I lift your name on high
Lord I love to sing your praises
I'm so glad you are in my life
I'm so glad you came to save us

You came from heaven to earth
To show the way
From the earth to the cross

### *Lord I Lift Your Name On High (Continued)*

My debt to pay
From the cross to the grave
From the grave to the sky
Lord I lift your name on high

Lord I lift your name on high
Lord I love to sing your praises
I'm so glad you are in my life
I'm so glad you came to save us

You came from heaven to earth
To show the way
From the earth to the cross
My debt to pay
From the cross to the grave
From the grave to the sky
Lord I lift your name on high

### *His Name is Wonderful*

His name is wonderful, his name is wonderful,
His name is wonderful, Jesus my Lord;
He is the mighty king, master of everything.
His name is wonderful, Jesus my Lord.

### *His Name is Wonderful (Continued)*

He's the great shepherd,
The rock of all ages,

Almighty God is he,
Bow down before Him, love and adore him.
His name is wonderful, Jesus, my Lord.

### *Father, I Adore You*

Father, I adore you,
Lay my life before you,
How I love you.

Jesus, I adore you,
Lay my life before you,
How I love you.

Spirit, I adore you,
Lay my life before you,
How I love you

### *He Has Made Me Glad (I Will Enter His Gates)*

I will enter his gates with thanksgiving in my heart.
I will enter his courts with praise.
I will say "This is the day that the Lord has made!"
I will rejoice for he has made me glad.

He has made me glad. He has made me glad.
I will rejoice for he has made me glad.
He has made me glad. He has made me glad.
I will rejoice for he has made me glad.

### *As The Deer*

As the deer panteth for the water,
So my soul longeth after thee
You alone are my heart's desire,

And I long to worship thee.

You alone are my strength, my shield,
To you alone may my spirit yield
You alone are my heart's desire
And I long to worship thee.

You're my friend and you are my brother
Even though you are a King
I love you more than any other
So much more than anything.

## *As The Deer (Continued)*

You alone are my strength, my shield
To you alone may my spirit yield
You alone are my heart's desire
And I long to worship thee.

I want you more than gold or silver
Only you can satisfy
You alone are the real joy giver
And the apple of my eye.

You alone are my strength, my shield
To you alone may my spirit yield
You alone are my heart's desire
And I long to worship thee.

## *I Have Decided To Follow Jesus*

I have decided to follow Jesus,
I have decided to follow Jesus,
I have decided to follow Jesus,
No turning back. No turning back.

The world behind me, the cross before me,
The world behind me, the cross before me,
The world behind me, the cross before me.
No turning back. No turning back.

### *I Have Decided To Follow Jesus (Continued)*

Tho' none go with me, still I will follow,
Tho' none go with me, still I will follow,
Tho' none go with me, still I will follow.
No turning back. No turning back.

Will you decide now to follow Jesus?
Will you decide now to follow Jesus?
Will you decide now to follow Jesus?
No turning back. No turning back.

### *Holy, Holy, Holy! Lord God Almighty!*

Holy, holy, holy! Lord God Almighty!

Early in the morning our song shall rise to thee;
Holy, holy, holy, merciful and mighty!
God in three persons, blessed Trinity!

Holy, holy, holy! All the saints adore thee,
Casting down their golden crowns around the
glassy sea; Cherubim and seraphim falling down
before thee,
Who was, and is, and evermore shall be.

### *Holy, Holy, Holy! Lord God Almighty! (Continued)*

Holy, holy, holy! Though the darkness hide thee,
Though the eye of sinful man thy glory may not see; Only thou art holy; there is none beside thee,
Perfect in power, in love, and purity.

Holy, holy, holy! Lord God Almighty!
All thy works shall praise thy name, in earth, and sky, and sea; Holy, holy, holy; merciful and mighty!
God in three persons, blessed Trinity! Amen.

### *Praise to the Lord, the Almighty*

Praise to the Lord, the Almighty, the King of creation!
O my soul, praise him, for he is thy health and salvation!
All ye who hear, now to his temple draw near;
Praise him in glad adoration.

Praise to the Lord, Who over all things so wondrously reigneth, shelters thee under his wings, yea, so gently sustaineth!
Hast thou not seen how thy desires ever have been
Granted in what he ordaineth?

### *Praise to the Lord, the Almighty (Continued)*

Praise to the Lord, O let all that is in me adore him!
All that hath life and breath, come now with praises before him.
Let the Amen sound from his people again,
Gladly for aye we adore him.

### *He's Got the Whole World in His Hands*

He's got the whole world in his hands,
He's got the whole world in his hands,
He's got the whole world in his hands.

He's got the wind and the rain in his hands,
He's got the wind and the rain in his hands,
He's got the whole world in his hands.

He's got the tiny little baby in his hands,
He's got the tiny little baby in his hands,
He's got the whole world in his hands.

He's got you and me, brother, in his hands,
He's got you and me, brother, in his hands,
He's got the whole world in his hands.

### *Silent Night! Holy Night*

Silent night, holy night,
All is calm, all is bright
Round yon virgin mother and Child.
Holy Infant, so tender and mild,
Sleep in heavenly peace,
Sleep in heavenly peace.

Silent night, holy night,
Shepherds quake at the sight;
Glories stream from heaven afar,
Heavenly hosts sing Alleluia!
Christ the Savior is born,
Christ the Savior is born!

Silent night, holy night,
Son of God, love's pure light;
Radiant beams from thy holy face
With the dawn of redeeming grace,
Jesus, Lord, at thy birth,
Jesus, Lord, at thy birth.

## *Silent Night! Holy Night (Continued)*

Silent night, holy night
Wondrous star, lend thy light;
With the angels let us sing,
Alleluia to our King;
Christ the Savior is born,
Christ the Savior is born!

## *Hark, the Herald Angels Sing*

Hark! The herald angels sing,
"Glory to the newborn King;
Peace on earth, and mercy mild,
God and sinners reconciled!"
Joyful, all ye nations rise,
Join the triumph of the skies;
With th'angelic host proclaim,
"Christ is born in Bethlehem!"

Hark! the herald angels sing,
"Glory to the newborn King!"

Christ, by highest heav'n adored;
Christ the everlasting Lord;
Late in time, behold him come,
Offspring of a virgin's womb.
Veiled in flesh the Godhead see;

### *Hark, the Herald Angels Sing (Continued)*

Hail th'incarnate Deity,
Pleased with us in flesh to dwell,
Jesus our Emmanuel.

Hail the heav'nly prince of peace!
Hail the Son of Righteousness!
Light and life to all he brings,
Ris'n with healing in his wings.
Mild he lays his glory by,
Born that man no more may die.
Born to raise the sons of earth,
Born to give them second birth.

### *Go, Tell It on the Mountain*

Go, tell it on the mountain,
Over the hills and everywhere
Go, tell it on the mountain,
That Jesus Christ is born.

While shepherds kept their watching
Over silent flocks by night
Behold throughout the heavens
There shone a holy light.

### *Go, Tell it on the Mountain (Continued)*

The shepherds feared and trembled,
When lo! above the earth,
Rang out the angels chorus
That hailed the Savior's birth.

Down in a lowly manger
The humble Christ was born
And God sent us salvation
That blessed Christmas morn.

### *When I Survey the Wondrous Cross*

When I survey the wondrous cross
On which the Prince of glory died,
My richest gain I count but loss,
And pour contempt on all my pride.

Forbid it, Lord, that I should boast,
Save in the death of Christ my God!
All the vain things that charm me most,
I sacrifice them to his blood.

See from his head, his hands, his feet,
Sorrow and love flow mingled down!
Did e'er such love and sorrow meet,
Or thorns compose so rich a crown?

### *When I Survey the Wondrous Cross (Continued)*

His dying crimson, like a robe,
Spreads o'er his body on the tree;
Then I am dead to all the globe,
And all the globe is dead to me.

Were the whole realm of nature mine,
That were a present far too small;
Love so amazing, so divine,
Demands my soul, my life, my all.

### *The Old Rugged Cross*

On a hill far away stood an old rugged cross,
The emblem of suffering and shame;
And I love that old cross where the dearest and best
For a world of lost sinners was slain.

So I'll cherish the old rugged cross,
Till my trophies at last I lay down;
I will cling to the old rugged cross,
And exchange it some day for a crown.

Oh that old rugged cross, so despised by the world,
Has a wondrous attraction for me;

### *The Old Rugged Cross (Continued)*

For the dear Lamb of God left his glory above
To bear it to dark Calvary.

In that old rugged cross, stained with blood so divine,
A wondrous beauty I see,
For 'twas on that old cross Jesus suffered and died,
To pardon and sanctify me.

To the old rugged cross I will ever be true;
Its shame and reproach gladly bear;
Then he'll call me some day to my home far away,
Where his glory forever I'll share.

### *Christ the Lord Is Risen Today, Sons*

Christ, the Lord, is risen today, Alleluia!
Sons of men and angels say, Alleluia!
Raise your joys and triumphs high, Alleluia!
Sing, you heavens, and earth, reply, Alleluia!

Lives again our glorious King, Alleluia!
Where, O death, is now your sting? Alleluia!
Once he died our souls to save, Alleluia!
Where your victory, O grave? Alleluia!

### *Christ the Lord Is Risen Today, Sons (Continued)*

Love's redeeming work is done, Alleluia!
Fought the fight, the battle won, Alleluia!
Death in vain forbids him rise, Alleluia!
Christ has opened paradise, Alleluia!

Soar we now where Christ has led, Alleluia!
Following our exalted Head, Alleluia!
Made like him, like him we rise, Alleluia!
Ours the cross, the grave, the skies, Alleluia!
Amen.

### *Hail, Holy Queen, Enthroned Above*

Hail holy queen enthroned above,
Oh Maria.
Hail mother of mercy and of love,
Oh Maria.
Triumph all ye cherubim,
Sing with us ye seraphim.
Heaven and earth resound the hymn.
Salve, salve, salve regina.

Our life, our sweetness here below,
Oh, oh, oh, oh Maria.

***Hail, Holy Queen, Enthroned Above (Continued)***

Our hope in sorrow and in woe,
Triumph all ye cherubim

Sing with us ye seraphim
Heaven and earth resound the hymn
Salve, salve, salve regina.

***Immaculate Mary***

Immaculate Mary, your praises we sing
You reign now in heaven with Jesus, our King.

Ave, ave, ave Maria,
Ave, ave, ave Maria.

On earth, we your children invoke your fair name.

Your name is our power, your virtues our light,
Your love is our comfort, your pleading our might.

We pray for our mother, the church upon earth,
And bless, dearest lady, the land of our birth.

### *Let Us Break Bread Together*

Let us break bread together on our knees,
Let us break bread together on our knees.
When I fall on my knees with my face to the rising sun,
O Lord, have mercy on me.

Let us drink wine together on our knees,
Let us drink wine together on our knees.
When I fall on my knees with my face to the rising sun,
O Lord, have mercy on me.

Let us praise God together on our knees,
Let us praise God together on our knees.
When I fall on my knees with my face to the rising sun,
O Lord, have mercy on me.

### *Amazing Grace! How Sweet the Sound*

Amazing grace! How sweet the sound
That saved a wretch like me!
I once was lost, but now am found;
Was blind, but now I see.

***Amazing Grace! How Sweet the Sound (Continued)***

'Twas grace that taught my heart to fear,
And grace my fears relieved;
How precious did that grace appear
The hour I first believed.

Through many dangers, toils and snares,
I have already come;
'Tis grace hath brought me safe thus far,
And grace will lead me home.

The Lord has promised good to me,
His Word my hope secures;
He will my shield and portion be,
As long as life endures.

***What A Friend We Have in Jesus***

What a Friend we have in Jesus, all our sins and griefs to bear!
What a privilege to carry everything to God in prayer!
O what peace we often forfeit, O what needless pain we bear,
All because we do not carry everything to God in prayer.

### *What A Friend We Have in Jesus (Continued)*

Have we trials and temptations? Is there trouble anywhere?
We should never be discouraged; take it to the Lord in prayer.
Can we find a friend so faithful, who will all our sorrows share?
Jesus knows our every weakness; take it to the Lord in prayer.

Are we weak and heavy laden, cumbered with a load of care?
Precious Savior, still our refuge, take it to the Lord in prayer.
Do your friends despise, forsake you? Take it to the Lord in prayer!
In his arms he'll take and shield you; you will find a solace there.

### *What a Fellowship, What a Joy Divine*

What a fellowship, what a joy divine,
Leaning on the everlasting arms;
What a blessedness, what a peace is mine,
Leaning on the everlasting arms.

### *What a Fellowship, What a Joy Divine (Continued)*

Leaning, leaning,
Safe and secure from all alarms;
Leaning, leaning,
Leaning on the everlasting arms.

Oh, how sweet to walk in this pilgrim way,
Leaning on the everlasting arms;
Oh, how bright the path grows from day to day,
Leaning on the everlasting arms.

What have I to dread, what have I to fear,
Leaning on the everlasting arms?
I have blessed peace with my Lord so near,
Leaning on the everlasting arms.

### *Swing Low, Sweet Chariot*

Swing low, sweet chariot,
Comin' for to carry me home!

I looked over Jordan and what did I see,
Comin' for to carry me home!
A band of angels comin' after me,
Comin' for to carry me home!

## *Swing Low, Sweet Chariot (Continued)*

If you get there before I do,
Comin' for to carry me home,
Just tell my friends that I'm acomin' too,
Comin' for to carry me home.

I'm sometimes up and sometimes down,
Comin' for to carry me home,
But still my soul feels heavenly bound
Comin' for to carry me home!

## JEWISH

### *Adon Alom*

He is the eternal Lord, who reigned before any being had yet been created; when all was done according to his will, already then his name was King.

A-don o-lam, a-sher ma-lach be-te-rem kol ye-tsir niv-ra, le-eit na-a-sa ve-chef-tso kol, a-zai me-lech she-mo nik-ra.

Ve-a-cha-rei ki-che-lot ha-kol, le-va-do yim-loch no-ra, ve-hu ha-ya, ve-hu ho-veh, ve-hu yi-he-yeh be-tif-a-ra.

### *Adon Alom (Continued)*

Ve-hu e-chad, ve-ein shei-ni le-ham-shil lo, le-hach-bi-ra, be-li rei-sheet, be-li tach-lit, ve-lo ha-oz ve-ha-mis-ra.

Ve-hu Ei-li, ve-chai go-a-li, ve-tsur chev-li be-eit tsa-ra, ve-hu ni-si u-ma-nos li, me-nat ko-si be-yom ek-ra.

Be-ya-do af-kid ru-chi be-eit i-shan ve-a-i-ra, ve-im ru-chi ge-vi-ya-ti: A-do-nai li, ve-lo i-ra.

### *Ein Keiloheinu*

There is none like our God; there is none like our Lord; there is none like our King; there is none like our Deliverer.

Ein kei-lo-hei-nu, ein ka-do-nei-nu, ein ke-mal-kei-nu, ein ke-mo-shi-ei-nu.

Mi chei-lo-hei-nu? Mi cha-do-nei-nu?

Mi che-mal-kei-nu? Mi che-mo-shi-ei-nu?

No-deh lei-lo-hei-nu, no-deh la-do-nei-nu, no-deh le-mal-kei-nu, no-deh le-mo-shi-ei-nu.

### *Ein Keiloheinu (Continued)*

Ba-ruch E-lo-hei-nu, ba-ruch A-do-nei-nu, ba-ruch Mal-kei-nu, ba-ruch Mo-shi-ei-nu.

A-ta hu E-lo-hei-nu, a-ta hu A-do-nei-nu, A-ta hu Mal-kei-nu, a-ta hu Mo-shi-ei-nu.

### *Lecha Dodi*

Beloved, come to meet the bride; beloved, come to greet Shabbat.

Enter in peace, O crown of your husband; enter in gladness, enter in joy. Come to the people that keeps its faith. Enter, O Bride! Enter, O Bride!

Refrain: L'kha dodi likrat kallah, p'nei Shabbat n'kab'la.

Shamor v'za-khor b'di-bur ekhad, Hish-mi-anu eil ham-yu-khad, Adonai e-khad u-sh'mo e-khad, L'sheim ul'tif-eret v'lit-hi-la.

Refrain: L'kha...

Likrat Shabbat l'khu v'neil-kha, Ki hi m'kor hab-ra-kha,

Mei-rosh mi-ke-dem n'su-kha, Sof ma-a-seh b'makh-sha-va, te-khi-la.

## *Lecha Dodi (Continued)*

Refrain: L'kha...

Ya-min us-mol tif-rotzi, v'et Adonai ta-aritzi.

Al yad ish ben par-tzi, v'nis-m'kha v'na-gila.

Refrain: L'kha...

(We rise and face the door to welcome the Shabbat bride.)

Bo'i v'shalom a-teret ba-la, Gam b'simkha uv-tza-ha-la

Tokh emu-nei am s'gu-la, (bow twice to the Shabbat bride)

Bo'i kallah, Bo'i kallah.

Refrain: L'kha...

## *Shalom Aleichem*

Peace be unto you, O ministering angels, messengers of the Most High, the supreme King of kings, the Holy One, blessed is He.

Sha-lom a-lei-chem, mal-a-chei ha-sha-reit, mal-a-chei El-yon, mi-me-lech ma-le-chei ha-me-la-chim, ha-ka-dosh ba-ruch Hu.

Bo-a-chem le-sha-lom…

Ba-re-chu-ni le-sha-lom…

Tsei-te-chem le-sha-lom…

## Patriotic

### *America the Beautiful*

O beautiful for spacious skies,
For amber waves of grain;
For purple mountain majesties
Above the fruited plain!
America! America!
God shed his grace on thee,
And crown thy good with brotherhood,
From sea to shining sea.

O beautiful for heroes proved
In liberating strife,
Who more than self their country loved,
And mercy more than life!
America! America!
May God thy gold refine,
Till all success be nobleness,
And every gain divine.

### *America the Beautiful (Continued)*

O beautiful for patriot dream
That sees beyond the years
Thine alabaster cities gleam,
Undimmed by human tears!
America! America!

God mend thine every flaw,
Confirm thy soul in self control,
Thy liberty in law.

### *Eternal Father, Strong to Save*

Eternal Father, strong to save,
Whose arm hath bound the restless wave,
Who biddest the mighty ocean deep
Its own appointed limits keep;

Oh, hear us when we cry to thee,
For those in peril on the sea!

O Christ! Whose voice the waters heard
And hushed their raging at thy Word,
Who walked on the foaming deep,
And calm amidst its rage didst sleep;
Oh, hear us when we cry to thee,
For those in peril on the sea!

### *Eternal Father, Strong to Save (Continued)*

Most Holy Spirit! Who didst brood
Upon the chaos dark and rude,
And bid its angry tumult cease,
And give, for wild confusion, peace;
Oh, hear us when we cry to Thee,
For those in peril on the sea!

O Trinity of love and power!
Our family shield in danger's hour;
From rock and tempest, fire and foe,
Protect us wheresoever we go;
Thus evermore shall rise to thee
Glad hymns of praise from land and sea.

*Alternate verse*

Lord, guard and guide the men who fly
Though the great spaces in the sky.
Be with them always in the air,
In darkening storms or sunlight fair;
Oh, hear us when we lift our prayer,
For those in peril in the air!

*Marine Corps' Verse*

Eternal Father, grant, we pray, to all Marines, both night and day, the courage, honor, strength, and skill, their land to serve, thy law fulfill; be thou the shield forevermore, from every peril to the Corps.

—J. E. Seim

# REFLECTIONS

Treat people as if they were what they ought to be and you help them to become what they are capable of being.

—Goethe

The significant problems we face cannot be solved at the same level of thinking we were at when we created them.

—Albert Einstein

That which we obtain too easily, we esteem too lightly. It is dearness only which gives everything its value. Heaven knows how to put a proper price on its goods.

—Thomas Paine

I slept and dreamt that life was joy.
I awoke and saw that life was service.
I acted and behold, service was joy.

—Rabindranath Tagore

A brave man risks his life but not his conscience.

—John Paul II

Civilization is always in danger when those who have never learned to obey are given the right to command.

—Bishop Fulton J. Sheen

A sound body is good; a sound mind is better; but a strong and clean character is better than either.

—Theodore Roosevelt

We shall not cease from exploration and at the end of all our exploring will be to arrive where we started and know the place for the first time.

—T.S. Eliot

A man should carry two stones in his pocket. On one should be inscribed, 'I am but dust and ashes.' On the other, 'For my sake the world was created.' And he should use each stone as he needs it.

—Rabbi Bunam

Prayer enlarges the heart until it is capable of containing God's gift of Himself.

—Mother Teresa

The great use of life is to spend it for something that outlasts it.

—William James

All that is essential for the triumph of evil is that good men do nothing.

—Edmund Burke

One man can make a difference and every man should try.

—John F. Kennedy

I believe in the sun even when it is not shining.

I believe in love even when not feeling it.

I believe in God even when He is silent.

(Inscription in a Cologne cellar where Jews hid in time of persecution.)

Do all the good you can, by all the means that you can, in all the ways you can, in all the places you can, at all the times you can, to all the people you can, as long as ever you can.

—John Wesley

A bad habit is first a caller, then a guest, and at last a master.

—Talmud

Hatred is like an acid; it can do more damage to the container in which it is stored than to the object on which it is poured.

—Ann Landers

There is no end to the good which one can do if he does not care who gets the credit.

—Anonymous

He who cannot laugh at himself always appears ridiculous.

—Dr. Larry T. McGehee

The trouble with most people these days is that they want to reach the Promised Land without going through the wilderness.

—Anonymous

No man is free if he fears death.

—Martin Luther King

Do not pray for easy lives. Pray to be stronger men! Do not pray for tasks equal to your powers. Pray for power equal to your tasks.

—Phillips Brooks

The block of granite which was an obstacle in the pathway of the weak becomes a stepping stone in the pathway of the strong.

—Carlyle

Life, if you know how to use it, is long enough.

—Seneca

Only those who learn how to live with loneliness can come to know themselves and life.

—Carl Sandburg

Love is not blind—it sees more, not less. But because it sees more, it is willing to see less.

—Rabbi Julius Gordon

Pray as though everything depended on God. Work as though everything depended on you.

—St. Augustine

It is easy to dodge our responsibilities, but we cannot dodge the consequences of dodging our responsibilities.

—Josiah Stamp

One thing I know, the only ones among you who will be really happy are those who will have sought and found how to serve.

—Albert Schweitzer

# REFERENCES

### SCRIPTURES

All Scriptures used in this Devotional Field Book are from the New International Version.

### PRAYERS

"The Marine's Prayer", used by permission of the Marine Corps Association.

"For Team Spirit", page 39.

Used by permission of C.R. Duncan.

"Self-Dedication", page 39. Reprinted from Lutheran Book of Worship, copyright 1978, by permission of Augsburg Publishing House.

"For those in our Country's Service in Time of War", page 39.

Reprinted from Service Book and Hymnal, copyright 1958, by permission of Augsburg Publishing House.

"Confession for the Critically Ill", page 51.
Reprinted from Prayer Book for Jewish Personnel
in the Armed Forces of the United States. Used by
permission of the Jewish Welfare Board.

"The Rosary", page 44. Reprinted with permission
from Everyday Catholic Prayers, copyright 1979,
Liguori Publications, One Liguori Drive, Liguori,
Missouri 63057, and the Apostolic letter of Pope
John Paul II.

"Stations of the Cross", page 45. Reprinted from
The Way of the Cross. Used by permission of
Barton-Colton, Incorporated.

"Evening Prayer", page 46. Reprinted from My
Hospital Prayer Book. Used by permission of St.
Francis Hospital, Milwaukee, WI.

"Christopher Prayer", page 47. Used by
permission of The Christopher, 12 E. 48th St., New
York, New York 10017.

"Two Orthodox Prayers", page 48. Used by
permission of the Department of Religious
Education of the Orthodox Church in America.

"Islamic Prayer", page 53. From collection of LT Abuhena Saifulislam, CHC, USN.

"Buddhist Meditation", page 54. From the Buddhist Churches of America.

## MUSIC

*As The Deer*, *Father I Adore You*, *He Has Made Me Glad*, *Lord I Lift Your Name On High*, used courtesy of Maranatha Praise, Inc. Administered by the THE COPYRIGHT COMPANY.

*His Name Is Wonderful*, use courtesy of Manna Music, Inc.

## STATEMENTS OF FAITH

"Jewish Statement of Faith," page 49. Reprinted from Prayer Book for Jewish Personnel in the Armed Forces of the United States. Used by permission of the Jewish Welfare Board.

Made in United States
Orlando, FL
30 December 2024